What's the Issue?

WHAT'S UNIVERSAL HEALTH CARE?

By Lorraine Harrison

KidHaven PUBLISHING

Published in 2019 by
KidHaven Publishing, an Imprint of Greenhaven Publishing, LLC
353 3rd Avenue
Suite 255
New York, NY 10010

Designer: Andrea Davison-Bartolotta
Editor: Katie Kawa

Photo credits: Cover (bottom) Monkey Business Images/Shutterstock.com; cover (top) NICHOLAS KAMM/AFP/Getty Images; pp. 5, 18 (left) J. Bicking/Shutterstock.com; p. 7 Buena Vista Images/ Photonica World/Getty Images; p. 9 Zoezoe33/Shutterstock.com; p. 11 (inset) Iuri Silvestre/ Shutterstock.com; pp. 11 (main), 19 (left) Mark Van Scyoc/Shutterstock.com; p. 13 Tana888/ Shutterstock.com; p. 15 Gino Santa Maria/Shutterstock.com; p. 17 SAUL LOEB/AFP/Getty Images; p. 18 (right) miker/Shutterstock.com; p. 19 (right) Drop of Light/Shutterstock.com; p. 20 Spencer Platt/Getty Images; p. 21 Apostrophe/Shutterstock.com.

Cataloging-in-Publication Data

Names: Harrison, Lorraine.
Title: What's universal health care? / Lorraine Harrison.
Description: New York : KidHaven Publishing, 2019. | Series: What's the issue? | Includes glossary and index.
Identifiers: ISBN 9781534525962 (pbk.) | 9781534525955 (library bound) | ISBN 9781534525979 (6 pack) | ISBN 9781534525986 (ebook)
Subjects: LCSH: Medical care–United States–Juvenile literature.National health insurance–United States–Juvenile literature. | Health services accessibility–United States–Juvenile literature.
Classification: LCC RA395.A3 H37 2019 | DDC 368.3'8'00973–dc23

Printed in the United States of America

CPSIA compliance information: Batch #BS18KL: For further information contact Greenhaven Publishing LLC, New York, New York at 1-844-317-7404.

Please visit our website, www.greenhavenpublishing.com. For a free color catalog of all our high-quality books, call toll free 1-844-317-7404 or fax 1-844-317-7405.

CONTENTS

Health Care for Everyone

When people get sick or hurt, they often go to a doctor. However, going to a doctor costs money, and some people can't afford it. This often happens when people don't have health insurance, which covers part or all of a person's **medical** bills.

Many countries have systems that allow everyone to get the health care they need without having to worry if they can afford it. This is called universal health care. The United States doesn't have universal health care. Some people believe that's a good thing, but others want to make universal health care a **reality** for Americans.

Facing the Facts 🔍

Universal health care is sometimes called universal health coverage (UHC).

Understanding different systems of health care can be **confusing**. However, it's good to know the facts about universal health care because people have such strong feelings about it.

The Right to Health Care

People who support universal health care believe no one should have to go without needed medical care because it's too expensive. They also believe a person should never be forced to live in **poverty** because they had to spend too much money on medical bills.

Many groups, such as the World Health Organization (WHO), want to bring universal health care to every country in the world. The leaders of these groups believe everyone should have the right to good medical care, which can allow them to live healthier, longer lives.

Facing the Facts 🔍

According to the WHO, paying for health care forces around 100 million people each year into extreme poverty, which means they have to live on less than $1.90 per day.

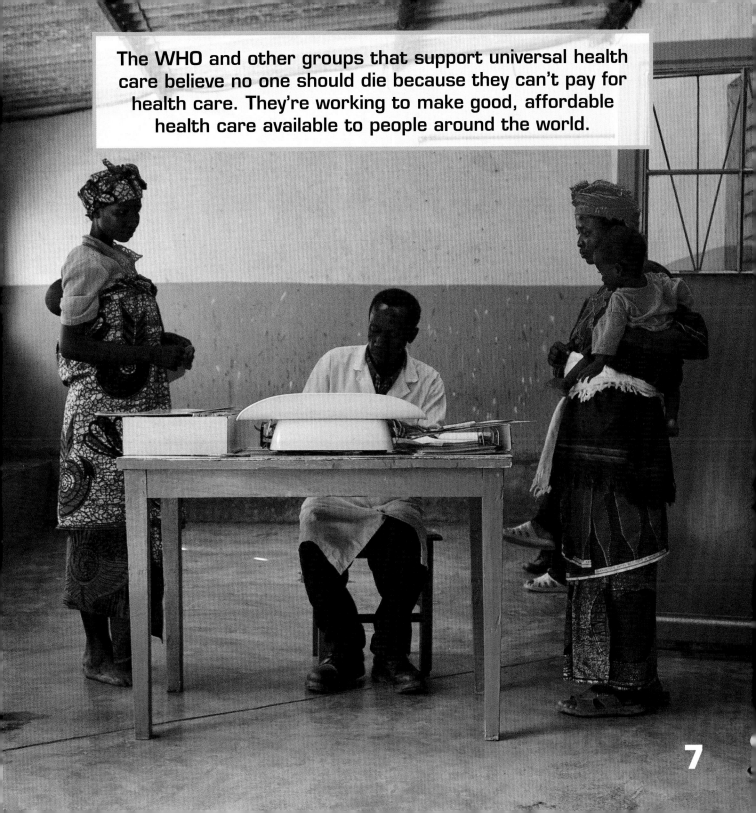

The WHO and other groups that support universal health care believe no one should die because they can't pay for health care. They're working to make good, affordable health care available to people around the world.

Single-Payer and Multi-Payer

Universal health care systems generally fall into one of two main groups. A single-payer system means that one group provides the money for health care for all the people in a country. Most often, that group is the government.

A multi-payer system also provides universal health care, but doctors and hospitals are paid by more than one group. These groups can include the government and different insurance companies. People can also buy extra insurance because not every medical service is covered by these systems.

Facing the Facts

In the United States, people most often get health insurance from private companies. They can buy it themselves or get it through their job, which means money for it is taken out of their paycheck.

Kinds of Health Coverage

What's it called?	What does it mean?	What's a country that has it?
single-payer	One group—often the government—pays for all health care services.	Canada
multi-payer	Doctors and hospitals are paid by more than one group, including the government and private companies.	France
health insurance mandate	A person must have health insurance, and if they can't afford it, they're given money to help pay for it.	Switzerland
private insurance	People pay for their own health insurance directly or through their job.	United States

This chart explains the most common health coverage systems in the world. All of them are examples of universal health care, except private insurance.

Where Does the Money Come From?

Universal health care isn't free. Doctors, nurses, and other medical staff still need to be paid. The money to pay them generally comes from the government in a single-payer system, but how does the government get that money?

The most basic way a government gets money is through taxes that citizens pay. Taxes generally **fund** a large part of universal health care systems around the world. Some people in the United States don't want to pay higher taxes, which is why they don't support universal health care.

Facing the Facts

Socialized medicine is a national health care system in which the government runs hospitals, provides jobs for doctors, and pays for health care for citizens. The National Health Service in England is one example of socialized medicine.

The WHO has come up with a plan to help countries pay for universal health care. Its goal is to have universal health care in every country by 2030.

Coverage Around the World

Many countries around the world have some kind of universal health care system in place for their citizens. This is especially true in industrialized countries, which are countries that use advanced **technology** to make many goods and provide many services. These countries are also known as developed countries.

The United States is one of the only industrialized countries that doesn't have a universal health care system in place. However, support among Americans for single-payer, universal health coverage is growing, according to a 2017 study.

Facing the Facts

As of 2013, people in the United States paid more money in taxes for health care than people in many countries that have universal health care systems, such as Canada and the United Kingdom.

Developed countries around the world have different health care systems, but most of them provide coverage for all citizens.

Health Care Help in the United States

Although the United States doesn't have universal health care, the U.S. government does fund some health care systems for certain groups of people. Two of those systems are Medicaid and Medicare, which were both started in 1965 by President Lyndon B. Johnson.

Medicare provides health coverage for people 65 years old or older, as well as younger people with disabilities. Medicaid provides health coverage for people of all ages who don't make enough money to pay for basic health care. These **programs** are paid for with help from taxpayers.

Facing the Facts 🔍

As of October 2017, about 68 million Americans had their health care covered through Medicaid.

In September 2017, U.S. Senator Bernie Sanders **introduced** a plan to turn Medicare into a universal health care program called Medicare for All.

What's Obamacare?

Another step toward universal health care in the United States happened in March 2010 when President Barack Obama signed the Patient Protection and Affordable Care Act (PPACA) into law. It's most commonly known as the Affordable Care Act (ACA) and has been nicknamed Obamacare after the president who signed it.

One of the main goals of the ACA was to lower the number of Americans without health insurance. It **expanded** Medicaid coverage, and it also tried to make health insurance less expensive and easier to get for many Americans.

Facing the Facts

In 2017, the U.S. Congress voted to do away with the part of the ACA that required most Americans to have health insurance or pay a fine.

The ACA has helped move the United States closer to a universal health care system. From 2010 to 2016, the number of Americans without health insurance dropped from 48 million to 28.6 million.

The Universal Health Care Debate

Many Americans have strong feelings about the ACA and other plans to bring universal health care to the United States. On one side of the **debate** are people who believe the United States should join other industrialized countries in providing health care for all its citizens.

On the other side of the debate are people who believe a person should have the freedom to choose their health coverage and if they're covered at all. They believe the government should stay out of health care and that taxes shouldn't be raised to pay for universal health coverage.

Some U.S. leaders, such as Speaker of the House of Representatives Paul Ryan (left) and President Donald Trump (right), have spoken out against the ACA.

Facing the Facts

In a 2017 study, 60 percent of Americans said they believe it's the government's job to make sure all Americans have health coverage.

Making Informed Choices

Health care systems are often hard to understand, but people are working in the United States and around the world to make it easier. Learning the most important facts about health care and how it's covered can help people make educated choices about their health.

Many people believe the best way to make sure citizens are healthy is to create a plan for universal health care. Different groups have different plans for making this happen, but the goal is the same: to make sure every person is able to get good, affordable health care.

Facing the Facts

In 2016, 20 percent of Americans without health insurance were unable to get medical care they needed because it was too expensive.

WHAT CAN YOU DO?

Learn more about different health care systems and plans for universal health care.

Ask your parents or guardians about your health care coverage.

Write to your leaders about the importance of universal health care.

Remind your parents or guardians to take you to the doctor for checkups and to visit their own doctors to help your family stay healthy.

If you know someone who's having trouble paying for health care, help raise money for them.

These are just some of the ways you can stay **informed** about this issue and help make sure you and the people around you get the health care you need.

GLOSSARY

confusing: Hard to understand.

debate: An argument or discussion about an issue, generally between two sides.

expand: To make something bigger.

fund: To provide money for something

informed: Having knowledge or facts about something.

introduce: To bring forward to be considered or talked about.

medical: Relating to the way sicknesses and other problems with the body are treated.

poverty: The state of being poor.

program: A plan of action.

reality: The way things actually are.

technology: A method that uses science to solve problems and the tools used to solve those problems.

FOR MORE INFORMATION

WEBSITES

HealthCare.gov Glossary

www.healthcare.gov/glossary

This website gives visitors helpful definitions for important health care terms.

KidsHealth

kidshealth.org

With pages for adults, teens, kids, and teachers, this website features everything a person needs to know about medical problems and staying healthy.

BOOKS

Braun, Eric. *Taking Action to Improve People's Health*. Minneapolis, MN: Lerner Publishing Group, 2017.

Carmichael, L. E. *Innovations in Health*. New York, NY: Crabtree Publishing Company, 2017.

Marsico, Katie. *The World Health Organization*. Ann Arbor, MI: Cherry Lake Publishing, 2015.

INDEX